ANCIENT ROME

Anne Millard

Illustrated by Joseph McEwan
and Roger Mann

Designed by Kim Blundell
Edited by Jane Chisholm

Contents

- 3 About this Book
- 4 Introduction to Ancient Rome
- 6 City Life
- 8 Shopping
- 10 A Town House
- 11 In the Kitchen
- 12 Eating
- 14 Furniture
- 16 Clothes
- 18 Hair and Beauty
- 20 Growing up in Ancient Rome
- 22 The Baths
- 24 The Games
- 26 Music, Dancing and the Theatre
- 28 Sports and Games
- 29 Chariot Racing
- 30 Villas and Gardens
- 32 Farming
- 34 People's Jobs
- 36 Building
- 38 Religion and Beliefs
- 40 Festivals
- 41 Family Customs
- 42 Slaves and Citizens
- 43 The Government
- 44 Professions and Learning
- 46 The Army
- 50 Travel and Transport
- 52 Architecture
- 54 Gods and Goddesses
- 56 The City of Rome
- 58 The Roman Empire
- 60 The History of Ancient Rome
- 62 Museums and Sites
- 63 Index

First published in 1981.
Corrected reprint published in 1987 by Usborne Publishing Ltd,
20 Garrick Street, London WC2E 9BJ, England.

Copyright © 1981, 1987 Usborne Publishing Ltd.

The name Usborne and the device are trade marks of Usborne Publishing Ltd.

All rights reserved. No part of this publication may be reproduced, stored in a retrieval system, or transmitted by any means, electronic, mechanical, photocopying, recording, or otherwise, without the prior permission of the publisher.

Printed in Italy.

About this Book

The world of the Ancient Romans is brought to life by the hundreds of colourful pictures in this pocket guide. It is full of scenes, like the one above of a Roman dinner party, which have been carefully reconstructed from archaeological evidence and other historical sources.

Some of the scenes include reconstructions of buildings, such as villas, flats or temples. Many of these are based on buildings which are now in ruins. A few, like the Pantheon, a temple in Rome (shown above), have been preserved almost intact.

Sometimes, instead of a reconstructed scene, you will see a reproduction of a Roman painting, carving or mosaic, such as this one of street musicians. Mosaics are pictures made up of small pieces of coloured stone.

There are also detailed illustrations of things the Romans used, such as furniture, pottery, jewellery and weapons. Some are based on objects shown in paintings or described in books, but most show objects that have been found.

The two main periods of Roman history are the Republic and the Empire and you will come across these terms as you read the book. To find out more about them, as well as the politicians, emperors and other people mentioned, turn to the "History of Ancient Rome" on pages 60-61.

Dates are followed by the letters BC or AD. BC stands for "Before Christ". AD stands for *Anno Domini,* Latin for "in the Year of Our Lord", meaning the number of years after the birth of Christ.

You may want to see some Roman remains or sites for yourself. On page 62, there is a list of Roman sites you can visit and museums with good Roman collections.

Although the book concentrates on the city of Rome itself, much of the information applies to the lives of people throughout the Roman Empire. To find out what territories this includes, see pages 58-59.

Introduction to Ancient Rome

The history of Ancient Rome dates back to about 750BC and covers over 1,000 years. It started as a collection of small villages on a group of seven hills near the River Tiber in what is now called Italy. The villages grew together into the magnificent city of Rome, which conquered the rest of Italy and eventually acquired a huge empire, covering most of Europe and parts of the Middle East and North Africa. The territories conquered by the Romans were known as provinces. This book refers mainly to life in Rome and the surrounding areas in the first two centuries AD.

The people of Rome

As you read this book, you will often come across people referred to as citizens and slaves. The people of Ancient Rome were divided into citizens, who had many legal, political and other privileges, and non-citizens, who did not. Citizens consisted of plebeians (the lowest rank), *equites* (businessmen) and patricians (noblemen). Some non-citizens were free born, others were slaves or freed men and women (former slaves). Many slaves were prisoners of war.

How we know about the Ancient Romans

Archaeologists have excavated the remains of Roman towns, villas and other buildings, which have provided information about the way the Romans lived.

In Rome itself, remains of many of the buildings have survived and these give us a general idea of the way the city looked in ancient times. This is the forum as it looks today.

Two sites of ancient towns have been especially useful. In 79AD the volcano Vesuvius erupted: Pompeii was buried under a layer of ash and pumice; Herculaneum was engulfed by lava and mud. As a result, both towns have been preserved in good condition until the present day.

Paintings on the walls of some of the houses show portraits of the people, as well as scenes from everyday life and legends about Roman gods and goddesses.

Many of the works of Roman poets, authors and historians have survived in libraries. These give us detailed accounts of Roman life and important events in the history of Rome.

This chart shows you some of the most important dates in the history of Rome. You can find out more about Rome's history on pages 60-61.

Date	Event
753BC	Founding of Rome. Rome ruled by kings.
510BC	Expulsion of kings. Founding of the Republic.
264-146BC	Wars with Carthage.
214-146BC	Wars with Greece and conquest of Greece.
59-51BC	Conquest of Gaul (France).
55-54BC	Caesar's invasion of Britain.
46BC	Julius Caesar becomes dictator.
44BC	Murder of Julius Caesar.
31BC	Beginning of the Empire (or Imperial times). Augustus (Octavian) is first emperor.
43AD	Conquest of Britain begins.
286AD	Diocletian divides the empire.
324-337AD	Constantine reunites the empire.
410AD	Sack of Rome by the Goths.
476AD	Last western emperor is deposed.

City Life

Most people in Rome and other large cities lived in blocks of flats three or four storeys high. These were built round a central courtyard and usually had shops on the ground floor. People with money to invest sometimes built apartment blocks and rented them out. Rents were high, although some blocks were so badly constructed that they fell down within a few years.

In Rome, torch-carrying nightwatchmen patrolled the streets, to keep law and order and to check that buildings were securely locked.

Fire was a problem, as many people burned fires in open containers, called braziers. In 6AD, a police and fire-fighting force was set up, called the Cohortes Vigilum.

Water was carried in pipes from lakes and rivers to the towns. Aqueducts were built to carry the pipes across the countryside.

Most people got their drinking water from the public fountains in the streets and washed in the public baths.

People could pay to have pipes connected to take water to their homes. Some did this secretly to avoid paying.

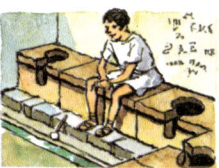
Many people used public lavatories, like these, though some apartments had their own lavatories on the ground floor.

The city's waste was carried in sewers under the streets. In Rome there was a huge sewer, called the Cloaca Maxima, which still exists today.

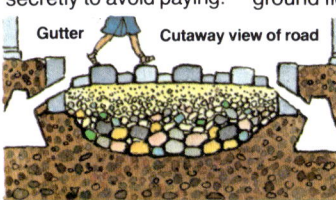
Pavements were raised up above the roads and there were stepping stones for pedestrians to use in wet weather. These also stopped carts from going too fast.

Many people had no kitchens of their own. They ate a lot of bread, which they bought from a public bakery.

Taverns and eating houses

People could also buy hot food and drink from eating houses and from stalls in the street. There were also taverns, where people went to drink wine and talk. Like the shops, these were often rooms, opening on to the street, on the ground floor of houses.

Shopping

Shop selling hot food | Butcher | Shop selling cloth | Pottery shop

Most Roman shops opened right on to the street, with a counter across the front. They were open early in the morning till late in the evening, with a long break in the afternoon.

Slaves were usually sent by their masters and mistresses to do the shopping for them. At night, wooden shutters were pulled across the shop fronts.

Shops selling olive oil were common, as it was used a lot both in cooking and for lamps. Some shops had their own olive press. The oil was stored in jars sunk in the ground.

The baker's shop usually had a mill at the back, where the flour was ground. The dough was made, then shaped into round, fairly flat loaves and baked in brick ovens.

To avoid traffic jams during the day, carts bringing goods to the market had to travel by night.

In Rome there were several markets, some specializing in a particular thing, such as meat or fish. In other towns, markets were held once a week in the forum, which was the centre of all business, political and legal activity in the town.

There were warehouses for storing goods. Some were built near the docks, so that boats could be unloaded easily.

Stallholders used scales called steelyards. The amounts were marked off along the bar. You could tell how much something weighed by moving the weight along until it balanced.

There were inspectors, called *aediles,* who checked the quality of the goods at the market and tested the weights and measures to make sure they were accurate.

Near the forum were the more fashionable shops, selling luxuries, such as books, perfume, fine cloth and furniture.

Traders who could not afford a shop or market stall wandered the streets, carrying their wares over their shoulders.

If a Roman wanted to borrow money, he could go to a moneylender or a banker, who charged high rates of interest on the money they lent.

Money

The earliest kind of Roman money was a rough bar of copper or bronze with an ox or cow on it. The Latin word for money, *pecunia,* comes from *pecus,* the word for cattle.

The first type of round coin was called an *aes grave* and was made of bronze. On one side was the two-headed god, Janus, and on the other, a ship.

After 200BC, silver coins were brought in – the *denarius,* and later the *sestertius* (or ¼ *denarius*).

During the Empire, a gold coin, the *aureus,* came into use. Emperors usually had their portraits on coins. This one is Augustus.

Political events were sometimes recorded on coins. The two sides of this coin refer to the murder of Julius Caesar on the Ides of March.*

Military conquests and other achievements, such as the building of the Colosseum (above), often appeared on the reverse side of a coin.

The Roman name for 15 March.

A Town House

Only the wealthy could afford to have their own houses in the centre of the town. They were usually built to the same basic design, with a small colonnaded garden at the back. At the front of the house was the *atrium*, or hall, where guests were received.

Houses had door handles and knockers made of bronze. These came from a house in Pompeii.

Here are some Roman locks and keys. As a precaution against thieves, doors were heavy and were securely locked.

Some houses had guard dogs too. "Beware of the dog" is the message on this mosaic, from Pompeii.

In the Kitchen

A rich man employed several cooks, each specializing in different dishes, and kept slaves to help them. Vegetables and sauces were cooked on wood or charcoal stoves and meat was roasted over an open fire. Most of the cooking was done in earthenware pots. They broke easily, but were cheap to replace.

Here are some Roman pots and cooking utensils. The tall jars, called *amphorae,* were used for storing wine and oil.

Wine was usually mixed with water, in a large bowl called a *crater*, before being served.

This cook is crushing spices and herbs in a mortar, using a club-shaped instrument called a pestle.

This bronze apparatus, rather like a tea urn, was used for keeping liquids warm (probably water or wine). The liquid went from the jar through a passage around the charcoal fire, and then out of the tap.

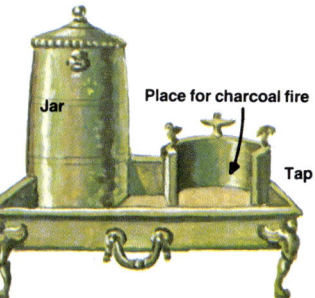

Eating

Poor people lived mainly on bread and a sort of porridge made of boiled wheat. Meat, fish and vegetables were expensive extras. Breakfast and lunch were both light meals. The main meal of the day was dinner. For wealthy people this sometimes lasted for several hours.

The Romans ate their food with their fingers, or with spoons. They did not use knives and forks.

Rich people had slaves to wipe their fingers clean for them between courses, using a bowl of water and a napkin.

A dinner party

In early times, men and women dined separately, but during the Empire, they were invited together. At dinner, the Romans lay on their sides on couches. Sometimes there were musicians and dancers to entertain the guests. It was also an occasion for poets and playwrights to come and read their latest works. Nine was considered the maximum number for a private party. Some Romans made it a habit to overeat and then make themselves sick, so as to have room to eat more.

Courses

The meal began with mixed hors d'oeuvres.

The main course consisted of various meat and fish dishes.

For dessert there were cakes made with honey, sweets, fruits and nuts.

Tableware

Here are some of the jugs, dishes and other things the Romans used at table. They were made of different materials – pottery, glass, bronze, silver or gold – depending on the wealth of the owner.

Roman glass ranged from almost transparent colours to thick, opaque glass with white patterns on a coloured background.

Every province had its own style of pottery. The most famous Roman pottery was Samian ware (above). Potters marked their goods, so we can trace where they were sold.

Furniture

Most ordinary flat-dwellers only had a few pieces of furniture, made of plain, rough wood. Furniture in more elegant houses was made of fine woods, bronze or marble and was often inlaid with silver, ivory, gold and tortoise-shell.

The Romans used chairs less than we do. They were kept mainly for women, old people or honoured guests. Instead, many people sat on stools, some of which could be folded. Some seats were upholstered and stuffed with wool.

Chests and cupboards were used for storing clothes and valuable objects.

The Romans ate from low, rectangular tables. Most houses also had small, ornamental tables, which were round or oval.

Statues and antique vases were displayed on tables or on special pedestals.

Couches were used at meals. They were high off the ground and often needed a stool to be reached.

Beds had leather or rope webbing, with a mattress of straw or wool. On top were blankets, a pillow and a bedspread.

Lamps

Roman houses were lit by oil-burning lamps. The oil was usually made from olives, nuts, fish or sesame seeds. Most lamps were made of pottery, but the more expensive ones were made of bronze and were very decorative.

Some lamps had small stands of their own, like this.

There were lanterns too, which were made to be hung from the ceiling.

A *candelabrum* was a tall stand for putting a lamp on. Some had branches, so that several lamps could be hung from them at once.

Heating

To keep their houses warm, people used braziers, like these, which burned charcoal.

Central heating

For those who could afford to have one, there was a central heating system, called a hypocaust. The floors of the houses were raised on pillars. A fire was kept burning in the cellar and the hot air passed between the pillars and heated the rooms above.

Clothes

Most Roman clothes were made of wool or linen, although cotton and silk were also worn. Men always wore white for official or formal occasions, keeping bright colours for parties.

A man's basic clothing was a loincloth and a tunic. If he were a citizen, he would also wear a toga – a large piece of cloth wrapped round the body.

Togas

Toga for parties · Senator's toga · Toga for mourning · Emperor's toga

Togas were normally white, but other colours were also worn. There were brightly coloured togas for parties and special occasions and dark togas for mourning. A senator's toga had a purple band and the emperor's toga was purple with gold embroidery.

Women's clothes

Clothing for women consisted of two pieces of underwear, an under tunic, with or without sleeves, and a dress, called a *stola*. A shawl, or *palla*, was sometimes worn on top.

Underwear · Tunic · Stola · Palla

A *stola* for wearing at parties was often embroidered or decorated round the hem.

Outdoors, respectable women wrapped themselves up well, keeping their heads covered.

Children's clothes

Children were dressed just like adults. A rich boy wore a *toga praetexta*, which had a narrow purple band.

For travelling, people wore cloaks of various designs.

Here is a selection of different styles of Roman sandals, shoes and boots. They were usually made of leather.

Jewellery

Rings were the most common item of jewellery. They were worn by both men and women.

A brooch, called a *fibula,* was used for fastening cloaks and tunics. Some looked very much like safety pins.

Cameos were used in a lot of jewellery. They are semi-precious stones with faces or figures carved in them.

Roman women wore gold chains and necklaces. They used a wide range of precious and semi-precious stones, but the most prized were pearls, opals and emeralds. Diamonds were not used as they were too hard to cut.

Here is a selection of styles of Roman bracelets. The snake design was popular and had been used earlier by the Greeks.

Most Roman women had pierced ears so they could wear earrings. The ones on the right consist of tiny beads threaded in bunches.

Hair and Beauty

In the early days of the Republic, men kept their hair and beards in short, simple styles. Later, beards went out of fashion for a time.

During the Empire, some young men wore their hair fairly long and kept it oiled and curled. Beards were also shaped in elaborate styles.

Rich men had their own slaves to cut their hair and shave them, but most ordinary men went to a barber's shop. This was also a place to meet friends and hear the latest gossip.

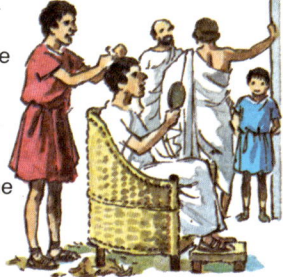

The Romans had several cures for baldness, some of which had very unpleasant ingredients. Some men preferred to wear wigs instead.

Women's hairstyles

In the early Republic, women usually wore their hair in a simple bun. By the beginning of the Empire, many new styles were worn, with plaits, curls and waves. Heated tongs were used to make the hair curl. Here is a selection of some of the styles.

Strips of cloth were sometimes used to keep the hairstyles in place. Wealthy women had jewelled circlets and diadems too.

Hair pins were also used. Some were made of carved ivory or gold and were worn as hair ornaments.

For a time it was fashionable to have fair or red hair. Some women dyed their hair or had wigs made from the hair of foreign slaves.

Roman women plucked their eyebrows with tweezers. Hair was rubbed off the rest of the body with a pumice stone.

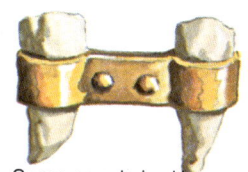
Some people had ivory false teeth fitted, like these. The Romans brushed their teeth with a special powder, rather like ground chalk.

This girl is pouring perfume into a flask. Roman men and women both used a lot of perfume, made from flowers, spices and scented woods.

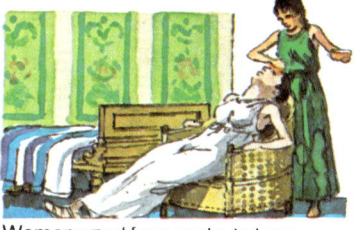
Women used face packs to keep their skin soft and free of wrinkles. One Roman face pack was made of flour and ass's milk.

Here is a selection of things a Roman noblewoman would have had on her dressing table. These mirrors are silver.

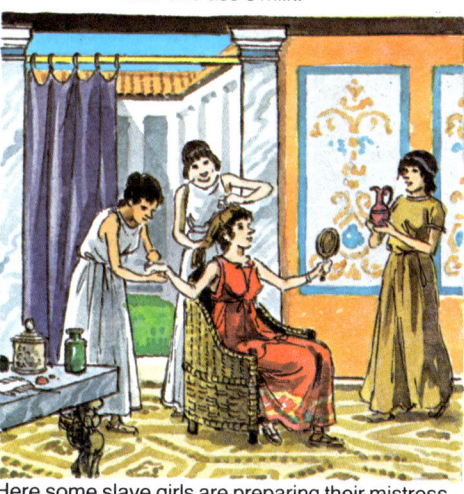
Here some slave girls are preparing their mistress for a party. Chalk is used as a face powder. Rouge is put on her cheeks, and her lips and nails are painted red. Her eyelashes and eyebrows are darkened and eyeliner is used. Roman make-up was made from vegetable and mineral dyes.

Growing up in Ancient Rome

In the early days, young children were brought up by their mothers. The girls were taught things like cooking and spinning.

From the age of seven, boys went out with their fathers to learn how to be farmers, craftsmen or soldiers.

Boys from well-off families were taught to read and write. They were trained for business or for an official career.

Later, wealthy women tended to hand over the care of their children to nurses and slaves.

When they were older, these children often had a private tutor, usually a Greek, to teach them.

Going to school

Although some children were educated at home, many others went to school – usually at about six or seven. They were taught reading, writing and simple arithmetic. Teachers were often strict and children were beaten if they did not learn their lessons.

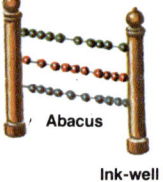

Young children wrote on wax tablets with a hard stylus. Mistakes could be rubbed out easily. The older ones wrote on papyrus, a kind of paper made from papyrus reeds. They used ink, and pens made of reed or metal. An abacus was used to help with doing sums.

At the age of twelve, very bright boys and ones from wealthy families went to a secondary school, where they were taught by a *grammaticus*. They studied Greek, history, geography, arithmetic and the works of famous authors.

If a young man wanted a political or legal career, he also had to learn oratory, the art of speaking in public.

To help students and schools, libraries were set up by the state or by rich men.

Keeping fit was an important part of Roman education, to prepare boys for the army. After lessons, they were expected to take part in sports, including running, wrestling and fencing.

Games and toys

School started early in the morning and finished in the afternoon. Then, children were free to go to the baths or play games. Games included rolling hoops and knucklebones, which was played rather like jacks.

Sometimes children pretended to be charioteers. They raced in small carts led by donkeys.

Dolls and model figures, like these, have been found in children's graves.

The Baths

There were public baths through the empire, but the ones in Rome were magnificently decorated with marble and statues. Many citizens spent much of the day at the baths, as they were free or cost very little. The baths were not just places to wash.

They had gymnasiums and gardens, and often shops and libraries too. People went there to meet their friends and talk. There were usually separate baths for men and women, although mixed bathing was allowed at one time.

First, you went to the changing rooms, where you left your clothes on a shelf. There was always a risk someone might take them.

Before bathing, people often took some sort of exercise, such as wrestling or weight-lifting.

The hottest room was the *laconicum*. Hot air passed under the floor and inside the walls. A vat of boiling water made the room steamy.

The *caldarium* was another hot, steaming room, which made people sweat a lot. It had a pool with hot water for bathing in.

There was a furnace in the basement to heat the water. Slaves stoked the fire constantly to keep it hot. The water passed from the tank to the baths in lead or clay pipes.

Instead of soap, the Romans rubbed oil on their bodies and then scraped it off with a stick called a *strigil*.

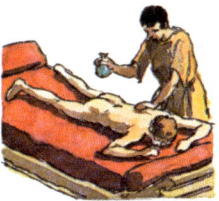

Some people took their slaves to the baths to do this for them, or hired a bath attendant.

After the hot bath, people often relaxed in the warm pool, called the *tepidarium*.

The cold bath, the *frigidarium,* was a large swimming pool – usually in the open-air. After a cold swim, you could relax by the poolside. For those who were hungry, there were often snacks for sale.

After the bath

For an extra fee, you could hire a trained attendant to give you a massage.

Barbers and hairdressers were often available. Slaves could be hired to provide beauty treatments.

For those with more serious interests, there were organized lectures and discussion groups.

There were gardens attached to the baths, where you could walk or meet your friends. For businessmen it was useful to find a quiet spot to discuss deals in private.

A large public baths might have had a library attached to it, so that people could study.

23

The Games

The Games was the name given to the fights and massacres that were held to entertain the Roman citizens. The idea began in 264BC, when two men staged a fight to the death between six slaves, as an offering to their dead father. Fights like this became very popular. They took place on public holidays, in honour of a god or a military victory.

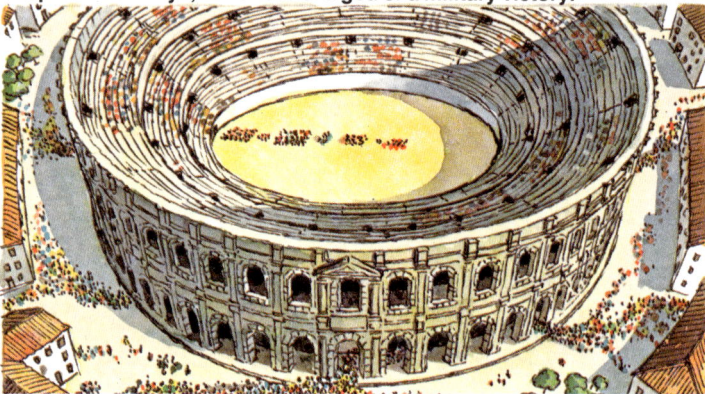

At first the audience watched from wooden stands, but later stone amphitheatres, like the Colosseum in Rome, were built. They were equipped with lavatories and eating houses. The Games always began with a procession. The gladiators (the men who fought) were accompanied by dancers, musicians, jugglers, and priests.

Gladiators were slaves, criminals or men who were in debt. They were trained in special schools, often by former gladiators.

To make the fights more interesting, there were different styles of fighting with different weapons and armour. The two gladiators on the right are dressed as a Samnite and a Thracian, enemies of the Romans. The man with a net and trident was called a *retiarius*.

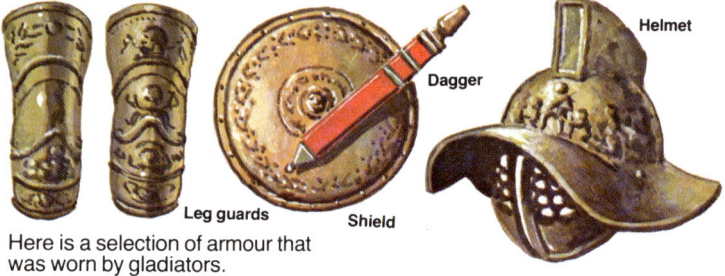

Here is a selection of armour that was worn by gladiators.

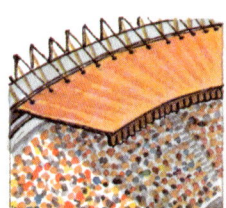
An awning, called a *velarium,* could be spread over the seating area, to protect the spectators from sun and rain.

Before the start of a fight, the gladiators greeted the emperor with the words, "Hail Caesar*, those about to die salute you".

The crowd decided the fate of a defeated man by praising or booing him. The emperor then signalled thumb up "let him live" or thumb down "kill him".

Successful gladiators became heroes and were rewarded with gold. If a gladiator won many fights, he might be able to buy his freedom.

Some gladiators were made to fight blindfolded on horseback.

Others were matched against wild animals, such as lions or tigers.

One of the most spectacular fights involved flooding the arena in order to reconstruct a naval battle, such as the one between the Athenians and the Persians.

Animals were imported from abroad and displayed in the arena. On one occasion herds of giraffe and ostriches were let loose, only to be hunted down by teams of archers.

Sometimes wild animals were set to fight each other to death.

On occasions, massacres were held in which Jews, Christians and criminals were killed by wild animals in the arena.

At the end of the fights the dead bodies were removed and sand spread everywhere, to cover the blood.

*Caesar was one of the emperor's titles.

Music, Dancing and the Theatre

Professional musicians and dancers performed at private parties, in theatres and before sporting events, such as racing or the Games. They were usually slaves or freed men and women.

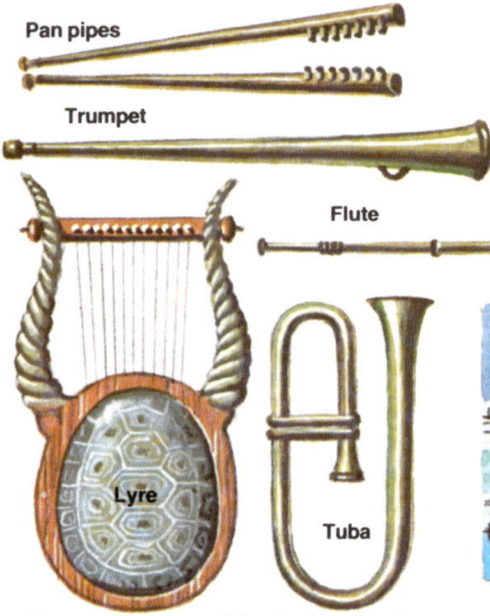

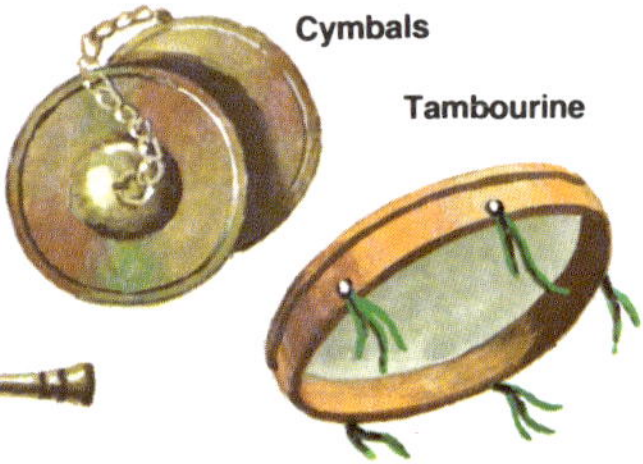

Here are some of the instruments that the Romans played.

Wealthy Romans, like this girl having a music lesson, learnt to sing and play instruments, but always remained amateurs.

Sometimes bands of travelling musicians, jugglers and acrobats performed in the streets.

By the time of the Empire, dancers entertained regularly at dinner parties. However, most Roman citizens did not dance themselves, as they thought it was beneath their dignity.

The theatre in Rome dated from 240BC, when they began performing versions of serious Greek plays. However, Roman audiences preferred comedies.

The actors always wore masks, to indicate the kind of character they were playing.

At first, plays were performed on temporary wooden stages. From the 1st century BC, permanent stone theatres were built. They were based on Greek theatres, although the seats were supported on a series of arches and vaults, instead of being cut into the slope of a hillside. Important people sat in wide seats at the front. There was a curtain drawn across the stage until the beginning of the performance.

Most of the actors were freed men. Here a group of actors are dressing for a play. At first only men were allowed on stage, so they acted the women's parts.

Some actors became very popular and received "star" treatment from fans.

In later tragic plays, the words were spoken by the chorus, a group of men who stood in the orchestra. The actors mimed. This kind of actor was called a *pantomimus*.

In comedies there were changes too. The actors stopped wearing masks and women were allowed on the stage.

Sports and Games

The Romans were generally more interested in watching sports than in taking part, but they believed in keeping fit. Each town had an exercise ground, called a *palaestra*, usually attached to the baths. Men practised running, jumping, wrestling and javelin-throwing.

Professional athletes were usually Greeks. They could be recognized by their hair, which was tied in a knot on top.

Boxers fought wearing *caestus*, spiked gloves that could inflict terrible wounds on the opponent.

The Romans played various kinds of ball games. Some people had special rooms in their villas for ball games.

In the countryside, Roman nobles sometimes went hunting wild boar or deer. Hunting dogs, like these, were imported from Britain.

Fishing was another popular sport. People fished along the river outside Rome, using a simple rod and line or a hand-net.

Romans played a lot of gambling games with dice, and board games using counters. These dice are made of ivory.

Knucklebones had originally been a Greek game. It was played with four pieces – bones or bone-shaped bits of glass, pottery or bronze. The pieces had numbers on each side. The player threw the pieces and then scored as we do with dice.

Chariot Racing

Chariot racing was popular all over the empire. In Rome there was an enormous stadium called the Circus Maximus, which held 250,000 people. The charioteers were usually slaves or freed men. The reins were tied round their waists, but they carried knives so that they could cut themselves free if they crashed. They wore helmets for protection. The charioteers were divided into four teams – the Reds, Blues, Greens, and Whites. The spectators bet on which would win.

Imperial box. The emperor and his family sat here.

The crowd cheered on their chosen team.

Taking corners was very dangerous.

The race was usually seven laps of the course. Bumping and ramming were allowed and added greatly to the excitement and danger.

The winner was awarded a purse of gold and treated as a hero.

Villas and Gardens

During the 1st century BC, it became the custom for wealthy Romans to build themselves magnificent villas on their country estates, or at fashionable seaside resorts. The villas were usually one or two storeys high and had large, beautifully laid out gardens, with fountains and pools.

This Roman painting gives us some idea of what a seaside villa would have looked like.

The gardens were decorated with sculptures and vases. This boy on a dolphin was part of a sculpture for a fountain.

The walls inside the villas were brightly painted, often with landscapes or scenes from stories of gods and heroes.

The floors were paved or covered with mosaics. The designs ranged from geometric patterns to scenes with animals or people.

Farming

In early times, most Romans were farmers, but by the end of the Republic, most farming was done on large estates with slave labour. People with small farms and no slaves were unable to compete. This is a villa on a fairly large estate. The most important crops were cereals, grapes and olives.

Growing wheat and barley

Before sowing seeds, the land had to be ploughed. Roman ploughs were made of wood tipped with iron.

Then the seeds were scattered over the ground. Wheat and barley were the two main cereals grown.

When harvest time came, the crops were cut with a sickle. Then the stubble was burnt and the fields ploughed again.

In Gaul (Roman France), a cart with knives in front was invented to cut the wheat.

Threshing – separating the grain from the straw – was done by driving horses round the threshing floor.

Then the grain was winnowed – separated from the chaff – and stored in sacks in barns on the farm.

Fruit and vegetables

Grapes were grown for fruit and wine. They were grown on trellises, picked and loaded into baskets, to be taken back to the farm.

To make wine, the grapes were put into a stone trough and then trodden in to extract the juice. The men held poles to stop slipping.

A press was used to squeeze out the last drops of juice. The juice was stored in jars, where it fermented and turned into wine.

Olives were grown in many parts of the empire. The oil was used for cooking, lighting and cleaning.

The Romans also grew fruit trees. This man is grafting a branch from one tree to another, to improve the quality.

Market gardens outside Rome kept the city supplied with vegetables, herbs, fruit and flowers.

Meat and fish

Farmers kept chickens, geese and ducks for their eggs and for meat.

Cattle, sheep, pigs and goats were all kept for eating. The milk from cows and goats was drunk or made into cheese. Cattle hides were used for leather. Here a farm worker is milking a goat.

Some estates had fish ponds, which were well stocked with freshwater fish for the table.

Hunting was another way of getting food. The Romans hunted deer, boar, hares, partridges, pheasants and pigeons.

Paying rent

Some farmers had no land of their own, so they rented it from wealthy landowners. They paid in money, crops or animals.

People's Jobs

In the early days of Rome, most citizens worked for themselves as farmers, craftsmen, traders or labourers. By the end of the Republic, many of these jobs were done by slaves. Many of the poorer citizens, or plebeians, were out of work. For the nobles, only jobs in the government, the army or looking after their estates were considered respectable ones. Most women worked in the home.

In Rome, each trade had its own club, or *collegia*, which held meetings and dinners. The members paid money into a fund, to pay for things such as their own funeral expenses.

A lot of people, mostly slaves, were employed in mills, grinding grain to make flour. The mills were usually attached to bakeries. In some mills the grinding was done by donkeys.

By the 1st century AD, the Romans knew how to use water wheels to drive mill stones, but they were rarely used.

Metalsmiths made tools, weapons and household goods, using bronze, iron and copper. Jewellers made brooches, rings and other ornaments, using gold and silver.

Early glass-makers moulded the glass into shape. By the 1st century BC, the Romans were using the technique of glass-blowing, which they had learnt in the Near East.

Carpenters were employed in many trades, including building and furniture-making. Many of their tools looked like the ones carpenters use today.

Boat-building was a trade that employed many slaves.

Potters made the containers for cooking, serving and storing food. Some estates had their own potters.

Cobblers made a whole range of footwear, from heavy nailed boots for the army to slippers and sandals.

The job of spinning and weaving cloth was mostly done by women at home.

Finishing off new woollen cloth was done by fullers. First the cloth was soaked in urine to thicken it.

To clean the cloth, it was trodden in a mixture of sodium carbonate and fuller's earth, a kind of clay. People also sent their togas to the fullers to be cleaned.

The cloth was then hung on frames over sulphur-burning fires, to bleach it. The fumes were poisonous and some fullers caught serious lung diseases.

After being washed, the cloth was combed with teasels or hedgehog skins. The fluff produced was used to stuff pillows.

The cloth was hung out to dry, then folded and flattened in a large press.

Slaves were not employed only as labourers. Educated slaves often had clerical jobs. Some former slaves worked in government service.

Some trusted slaves became business agents for their masters. In their spare time they could conduct deals of their own, and make money to buy their freedom with.*

*See page 42.

Building

The stone for building was cut from quarries, usually owned by the state. Large numbers of slaves were employed to cut and lift the stone. Cranes were used to lift the larger ones. Stone blocks were removed from the quarry wall by drilling holes and filling them with wooden wedges. The wedges were then soaked with water, causing them to swell and split the stone. It was sometimes sawn into smaller blocks.

With huge supplies of slave labour, the Romans were able to tackle many building projects. They built new towns, forts, bridges and aqueducts, many of which are still standing today. Cranes and scaffolding were used to raise the stone into place.

Arches and vaults

To build an arch, an arch-shaped wooden support was put at the top of two columns of stone. Wedge-shaped stones were placed in position around the support.

To build a vaulted ceiling, this process was repeated all the way along the passage.

Materials

Many houses and flats were built from wooden frames filled with stones and mortar, a kind of cement, and a layer of plaster on top.

The mortar, which dried as hard as concrete, was made by mixing lime, sand, water and gravel.

Bricks were often used in building. Roman bricks were thinner than ours. They were made of clay, shaped in wooden moulds and baked hard in a kiln.

Decoration

The walls of elegant houses were decorated with paintings, or murals. The artist applied the paint while the plaster was still wet.

Public buildings and private villas were adorned with marble statues and busts. Sculptors and stone masons were hired to make them.

Floors were sometimes decorated with mosaics, pictures of patterns made from small pieces of coloured stone.

The mosaic maker worked from a plan. First he spread wet plaster over a small area of the floor and smoothed it down.

Then he pressed the pieces of stone into the plaster, making sure he followed the design on his plan.

Building a bridge

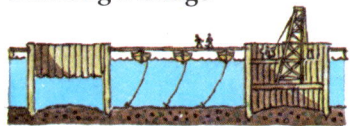

First a temporary bridge was set up across a row of boats. Wooden stakes, chained together in a circle, were driven into the river bed. The water was then pumped out of this enclosed area.

The area inside the stakes was filled with blocks of stone, which made the piers to support the bridge. When the piers were high enough, a wooden framework was hoisted into place between them.

Religion and Beliefs

For most people, religious life was based in the home. Each house had a shrine. Family ceremonies were held there and daily prayers were said to Vesta, goddess of the hearth.

In the shrine were figures of the Lares and Penates, spirits that guarded the family and the home.

Temples

This is what a Roman temple looked like. Each temple was dedicated to the worship of a particular god or goddess, whose statue was kept inside. The temples did not hold religious services with a congregation participating.

Outside the temple was an altar, where sacrifices of animals were offered to the gods on holy days.

People visited the temple of their favourite god or goddess if they had a special problem or favour to ask.

In order to please the god they might burn incense, say prayers or make an offering of money or goods.

Priests and priestesses served in the temples. They were in charge of receiving people's offerings and making sacrifices to the gods.

The chief of all the priests in Rome was the Pontifex Maximus. From the time of the Emperor Augustus (left), this position was always held by the emperor himself.

The temple of Vesta

There were some round temples, like the temple of the goddess Vesta, the most sacred shrine in Rome. A fire was kept burning inside by the Vestal Virgins, who were in charge of the shrine.

Every five years, a new girl was chosen to be a Vestal Virgin and she served for 30 years. She was forbidden to marry, but was highly respected and had special privileges.

Fortune telling

The Sibyl was a priestess who lived in a cave and foretold the future. The Sibyl's predictions were written down and consulted in times of trouble by emperors and politicians.

Augurs were priests who interpreted thunder and the flight patterns of certain birds, to tell whether the gods were pleased or angry with their worshippers.

A priest called a *haruspex* gained similar information by examining the liver of a sacrificed animal.

Special sacred chickens were kept. If they ate greedily, it was a good omen. Bad appetites meant that the gods were angry.

The Romans also believed that events were foretold in the stars. Many emperors kept an astrologer to advise them.

Ordinary people often went to fortune tellers who told the future with special dice, or by going into trances.

Curing illness

People who were ill sometimes sought a miracle cure by sleeping in the temple of the god of medicine, Aesculapius.

Others tried bathing in sacred springs, wells or baths.

Festivals

The Romans had a lot of public holidays, or holy days, usually to celebrate the festival of a god or goddess. Great processions were held. Animals, paid for by the government, were sacrificed at the altar outside the temple. Festivals were also occasions for feasting and drinking and visits to the Games.

New Year was celebrated on 1 March. Fresh laurel leaves were hung on the doors of buildings and the Vestal Virgins lit a new fire in their temple.

One of the liveliest festivals was Saturnalia, the feast of the god Saturn, which was held in December. Slaves swapped roles with their masters and were waited on.

The Lupercalia, in February, celebrated the founding of Rome. This statue shows the legendary founder, Romulus, and his brother, Remus, who were nursed by a wolf.

The festival of Flora, goddess of flowers, lasted for a whole week. Tables were piled high with flowers and people danced around wearing garlands of petals.

Family Customs

In early times, a father could order that a weak or deformed baby be left outside to die. This was because he could not afford to bring up a child who would not be able to work or fight. Later this was stopped, though fathers still controlled their children's lives and chose their husbands and wives.

On the 8th or 9th day of its life, a child was purified, named and given a *bulla,* a charm of gold or leather.

When a boy reached manhood, there was a day of celebration. He put on the grown-up toga and dedicated his *bulla* at the shrine.

Weddings

A wedding began with a sacrifice and then the bride and groom ate a special cake. There was a procession in which the bride was led by children to her new home, where her husband was waiting to greet her. After more ceremonies, she was carried over the threshold.

Women's lives

In early times, Roman women had few rights but many duties. A woman was always in the power of a man, first her father, then her husband, and then, if she became a widow, her son. Divorce was forbidden. Later, things improved and women gained more control over their own lives.

Funerals

When a rich person died, they were dressed in their best clothes and laid in the *atrium* of the house. Friends and relations came to pay their respects. On the day of the funeral, a procession took the body to the forum. Then people made speeches about the dead person.

The corpse was burnt on a fire and the ashes were placed in a jar called an urn.

The urn was placed in a family tomb, which was outside the city boundaries. Then everyone had a feast.

Many people's ashes were put in urns in huge underground tombs, called catacombs.

Slaves and Citizens

At the bottom of the Roman social scale were the slaves. They were completely at the mercy of their owners. Those with some skills, or who worked as private servants for kind owners, could lead quite reasonable lives. However, many others worked as labourers in conditions which were so bad that they died young of overwork. Sometimes slaves tried to run away, but they were usually caught.

In the early days, there were few slaves and they were usually treated as part of the family. As the Roman Empire grew, thousands of conquered people were taken and sold at slave markets.

Slaves were sometimes given tips, which they could save to buy their freedom. Some masters gave away freedom to their favourite slaves.

When a slave was freed there was a special ceremony, called manumission. Some slaves were freed in their master's will.

Many freed men and women worked hard and did well for themselves as traders or craftsmen. Some were made citizens.

Citizens

Citizens had many privileges which were denied to non-citizens. Non-citizens did not have access to many of the facilities in Rome, such as the baths or the Games. Citizens were entitled to wear the toga, a mark of social status. Yet, many of the lowest rank, the plebeians, were poor and unemployed.

The government paid a "dole" of free grain and provided baths, races and the Games, to keep the unemployed citizens quiet and happy.

The next rank of citizen, the *equites,* had once been cavalry officers. During the Empire, most were rich businessmen.

The richest and noblest Roman families were the patricians. Only they could hold the highest government offices.

Rich Romans increased their prestige by a system of patronage. Poorer citizens became clients, visiting the patron regularly and receiving money, clothes and perhaps the offer of a job. In return, clients supported their patrons in elections or in court cases.

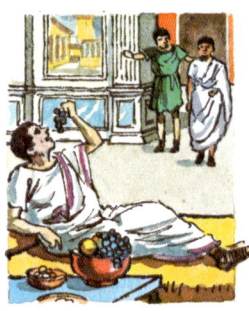

The Government

In Republican times, the Romans were ruled by a group of men called the Senate, who were chosen from the patrician class. Government officials were elected by all male citizens. In Imperial times, the emperor had power over the Senate, and appointed the officials.

The Senate was made up of 300 (later 600) men, called senators. They decided on government policies and how public money should be spent. Here a meeting of the senators is in progress.

The letters SPQR were written on military standards. They stand for "the Senate and the people of Rome".

The plebeians had their own assembly, where they could accept or reject the proposals of the Senate. After 287BC, their own proposals, *plebescita*, had the force of law.

The plebeians elected tribunes to look after their interests. Later, emperors took the title of tribune.

A political career

A well-born young man who wanted a career in the government usually began with a few years in the army.

His first official appointment was likely to be that of *quaestor*, a government official dealing with finance.

The next step was to become an aedile, supervising markets, public buildings and the Games.

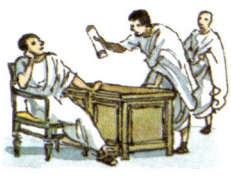

After that he might become a *praetor*, supervising law courts and making sure the laws were kept.

The highest postition was consul. The senators elected two consuls each year, to rule over the Senate.

An ex-consul could become a proconsul, governor of a province of the empire. Proconsuls were assisted by legates.

Professions and Learning

The Romans did not regard all professions equally highly. Teachers, for example, were looked down on and badly paid. Teaching was often done by Greeks. The Romans liked education to have a practical use. Lawyers were highly respected and law was considered a suitable training for a young man going into politics. Most authors and poets earned very little and depended on rich patrons, unless they had money of their own.

This is Virgil, one of the few well-paid Roman poets. He was author of the Aeneid, the story of the Trojan hero, Aeneas, and the founding of Rome.

A skill that the Romans regarded very highly was the art of oratory, or public speaking. It was essential for a political or legal career. This is the famous orator, Cicero.

Philosophers were also respected. People read their works and visited them to hear their teachings.

As printing had not been invented, books had to be written by hand. Booksellers employed slaves, usually Greeks, who could read and write, to do this.

Books were made by joining together sheets of papyrus – a kind of paper made from papyrus reeds. A stick was attached at one end and the papyrus was wound into a scroll, called a volumen. Later, books more like our own were made from sheets of vellum or parchment (both made from animal skin) folded and sewn together. This kind of book was called a codex.

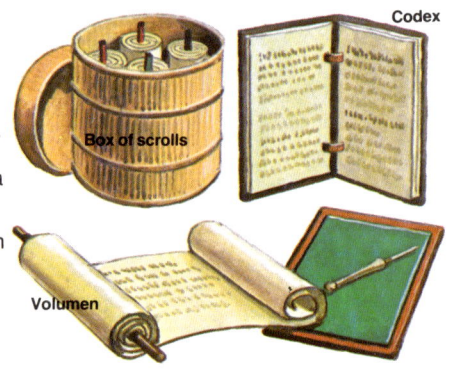

Law

Roman law was based on the "Law of the 12 Tablets", which had been drawn up in the 5th century BC, laying down punishments for basic crimes. Later, new rules were added to cover issues that had not been dealt with. Some laws were adapted from those of subject peoples of the empire. In the eyes of the law people were divided into *honestiores* (honourables), who were well off, and *humiliores* (dishonourables), who were poor. *Humiliores* usually got much harder punishments.

An accused man could defend himself in court or pay a professional lawyer to act for him.

Medicine

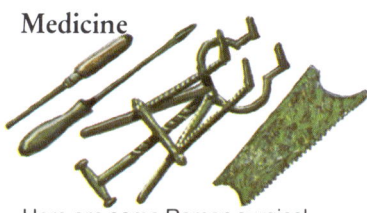

Here are some Roman surgical instruments. There were many skilled surgeons, but operations were risky, as there were no anaesthetics or antiseptics.

In early Rome there were no doctors. People tried to cure their families with home-made potions and traditional remedies. In the 2nd century BC, Greek doctors started coming to Rome and were paid well for their services. Besides medicines, they recommended balanced diets, fresh air, exercise, baths and massage. However, some doctors still tried to cure people with potions made from things like animal dung or gladiator's blood.

Numbers

These are the Roman numbers. When a number comes before one larger than itself, you subtract it, e.g. IV=4 (5−1). When a smaller number follows a larger one, you add, e.g. VII=7 (5+1+1).

I	II	III	IV	V
1	2	3	4	5
VI	VII	VIII	IX	X
6	7	8	9	10
XI	XII	XIII	XIV	XV
11	12	13	14	15
XVI	XVII	XVIII	XIX	XX
16	17	18	19	20
XL	L	XC	C	CC
40	50	90	100	200
CD	D	DC	CM	M
400	500	600	900	1000

The calendar

The Roman year began on 1 March, until 153BC, when it was altered to 1 January. The year was divided into 12 months, named after gods, emperors and numbers. The names we use are based on theirs. For example, March is named after Mars, July, after Julius Caesar and August after the Emperor Augustus. The year was 365 days long, but because they did not have leap years it started to get out of line with the seasons. Caesar corrected this in 45BC and in Britain it was not corrected again until 1752AD. The letters a.m. and p.m. stand for the Latin words *ante meridiem* and *post meridiem,* meaning before and after midday.

The Army

Almost constant warfare against their neighbours made the Romans experienced, efficient soldiers. In the early days, all property-owning citizens were expected to serve in the army, each providing his own weapons. Campaigns were usually held in the summer.

Hastatus or princeps · Triarius · Veles

The early armies had four kinds of soldiers. *Hastati* and *principes* were the younger, lighter-armed men. *Triarii* were older and more heavily armed. *Velites* were poor citizens with weapons but no armour.

Marius's reforms

Later, as the empire grew and much of the fighting took place abroad, a full-time professional army was needed. In the 2nd century BC the army was reformed by General Marius (left). He issued uniforms and weapons to all soldiers, and raised the pay.

Recruits were given rigorous training, which included marching, riding, swimming, fighting and building camps.

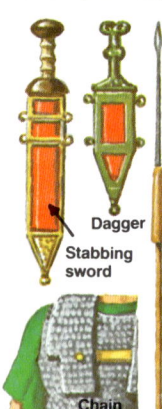

Dagger · Stabbing sword · Shield · Light pilum · Helmet · Chain mail shirt · Heavy pilum

Later, the chain mail shirts were replaced by armour made of segmented metal plates. In cold climates, the soldiers could wear breeches too.

Each soldier had a short stabbing sword, a dagger, a heavy and a light *pilum* (or javelin), a helmet, a shirt of chain mail and a shield. Each cohort (see next page) had a different coloured shield.

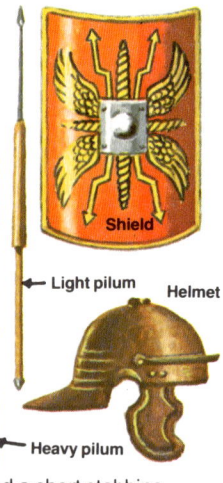

Senior officers had special made-to-measure armour made of moulded leather or bronze. This is Julius Caesar in his army uniform.

The organization of the army

The army was divided into legions. By the time of the Empire, there were 28 legions, each divided into ten cohorts. The First Cohort was the largest and had 800 men. The other cohorts had 480 men, who were divided into six centuries of 80 men each. Ordinary soldiers were called legionaries.

Some legions had special names and emblems. This is the running boar, symbol of the 20th Legion, called the Valeria Victrix.

Each legion was commanded by a legate and had a standard with an eagle on top, carried by an aquilifer.

Beneath the legate, there were six officers called tribunes. The senior tribune commanded in the legate's absence. Tribunes were often young men starting a political career.

The prefect of the camp was the third in command, after the legate and the senior tribune. He was in charge of equipment and engineering works, such as building camps.

Each century was commanded by a centurion. Other officers included the trumpeter, the standard bearer and the centurion's deputy.

Trumpeter

Centurion

Standard bearer

A century was divided into groups of eight men who shared a tent and ate together. This group was called a *contubernium*.

A troop of cavalry was attached to each legion. They acted as scouts and carried messages in battle.

Non-citizens could become auxiliary soldiers, attached to a legion. After 25 years, they were given citizenship and their sons could become legionaries.

Going to war

When the army went on campaign, each soldier had to carry his own equipment. This included weapons, tools, bedding, cooking pots and enough food for three days.

Each night they built a camp by digging a ditch around the tents. The earth thrown up from the ditch formed a rampart, into which they planted wooden stakes.

Here a doctor is at work on the battlefield. Camps and forts had well-equipped hospitals for the sick and wounded. As well as soldiers, the legions had their own doctors, clerks, priests, engineers, surveyors and labourers.

Discipline in the army was strict. There were punishments laid down for each offence, ranging from extra work to flogging and death.

Soldiers arranged their shields in a "tortoise" formation, like this, so that they could march safely towards the enemy.

The Romans were expert at siege warfare. They had catapults that could hurl heavy rocks and arrows at the enemy and battering rams to beat down enemy walls. Siege towers with drawbridges were used to climb on to the walls.

Although the soldiers were paid, taking booty was regarded as one of the rewards of capturing an enemy city or fort.

Defence

The Romans built permanent stone forts along their frontiers. Legions were posted there to guard the frontiers, keeping invaders out and maintaining law and order among the population.

Ships

The Emperor Hadrian built a great wall across the north of England, to defend the most northern part of the Roman Empire.

Roman warships ranged in size from biremes, which had two banks of oars, to quinquiremes, which had five. These ships were used mostly for transporting troops, though the Romans fought many sea battles with the Carthaginians of North Africa. Ships were also used to fight piracy.

The Empire

The Praetorian Guard were the emperor's bodyguards. They were paid well to ensure their loyalty.

There were several awards for bravery, such as medals and crowns. When soldiers retired they were given money or land.

After a victory, the emperor held a triumphal procession, or built an arch or column, to celebrate and to impress his subjects.

Travel and Transport

Travel throughout the empire was made easier by the excellent roads the Romans built. The roads were always straight, unless there was a serious obstacle, such as a mountain, in the way. This enabled the army to march swiftly to any trouble-spots. There were milestones every 1,000 paces. (A pace is equal to two steps and 1,000 paces is roughly 1,500m.)

Chariot carrying emperor's post.

Coach with many passengers.

Chariot

Most people travelled on foot. Those who could afford it went on horseback, in chariots, or in elegant carriages. For long journeys, people could hire large, slow coaches, with room for several passengers.

Rich man's carriage

There were wayside inns, where travellers could stop and rest or change their horses.

Overnight, people set up tents by the roadside. Rich travellers brought servants and guards with them.

Bandits were a constant danger, despite the army's efforts to keep the roads safe.

Travel in Rome

In Rome itself, wheeled vehicles were not allowed during the day, so the rich travelled in litters, carried by slaves. Some litters were made of rare woods, with fittings of gold, silver and ivory. Inside there were cushions and curtains.

Carts carrying heavy goods travelled by night. They were pulled by horses, mules or oxen.

Building a road

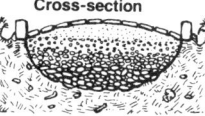

Cross-section

First, surveyors marked out the new road with stakes. They used an instrument called a *groma* (shown here), to make sure the land was level.

Then workmen dug a trench and laid stone kerbstones. Major roads were about 12m wide.

Firm foundations were built up from layers of sand, stone and pebbles. The top layer of stones was curved slightly, to drain off rainwater.

Sea travel

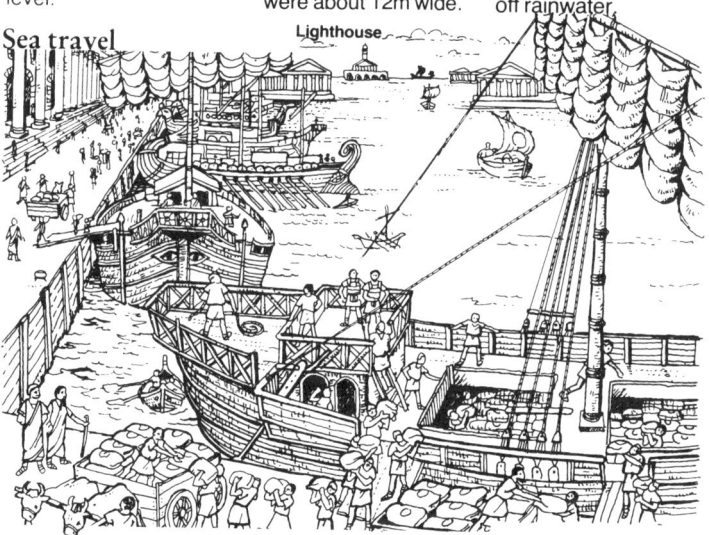

Lighthouse

The Romans traded with all parts of the empire and beyond. The goods travelled by sea, usually through the port of Ostia, on the coast near Rome. Pirates were a threat to shipping until patrolling warships, under General Pompey, got rid of them. By the time of the Emperor Augustus, about 120 ships sailed as far as India each year.

Heavy goods were often transported inland by river. Some river boats were towed, others could be sailed or rowed.

Some wealthy Romans were keen tourists and they visited places all over the empire, for their health, education or for a holiday.

Architecture

The Romans were very impressed by Greek architecture and borrowed not only Greek styles, but Greek architects and craftsmen too. For this reason, Roman architecture looks very similar to that of the Greeks.

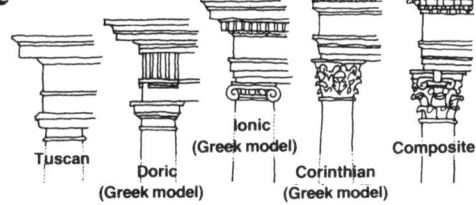

The Romans used five styles of column, adapted from the three that were used in Greek architecture. Columns were used for decoration as well as for support.

Roman temples looked very like Greek ones. They were mostly oblong with a triangular carved pediment and columns at the front. The temple was built on a platform, with steps leading up to it.

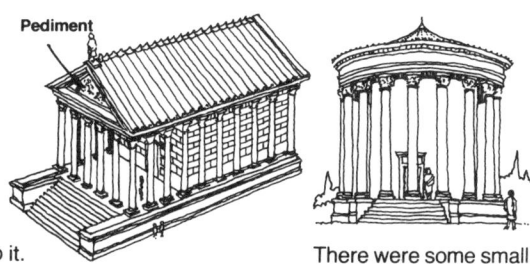

There were some small, round temples too.

Town planning

Whenever the Romans built new towns, they planned them on a grid, so that the streets were all at right angles or parallel to each other.

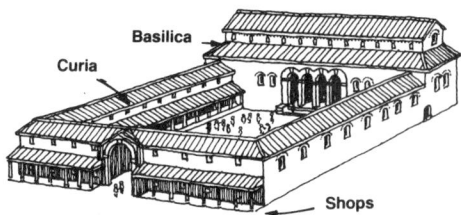

Each town had a forum, an open space where public meetings and markets could be held. Situated around the forum were shopping arcades, the curia (where the town council met), and the basilica (the law courts).

The basilica became the model for all the early Christian churches. It was usually rectangular, and had a central nave with a lower-roofed aisle on each side. The aisles were sometimes lined with columns.

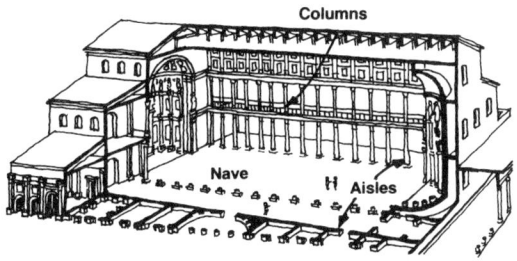

Arches, vaults and domes

Although the Romans did not invent the arch, they put it to greater use than anyone before them, building huge bridges and aqueducts all over the empire.

Triumphal arches, like this, were built in Rome and the provinces, to celebrate victories in battles.

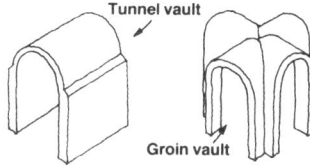

The tunnel or barrel vault was made simply by extending the arch, or building a series of arches, to make a tunnel shape. A groin vault was made by overlapping two tunnel vaults at right angles.

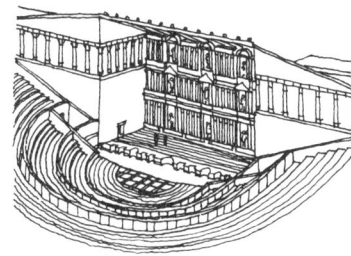

Roman theatres were built on flat ground and had arches and vaults to support the seats. In Greek theatres the seats had been built into the natural slopes of a hillside.

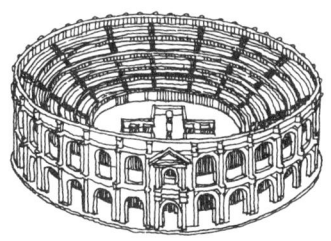

The Romans applied the same technique to building amphitheatres, the round and oval stadiums in which gladiator fights and chariot races were held.

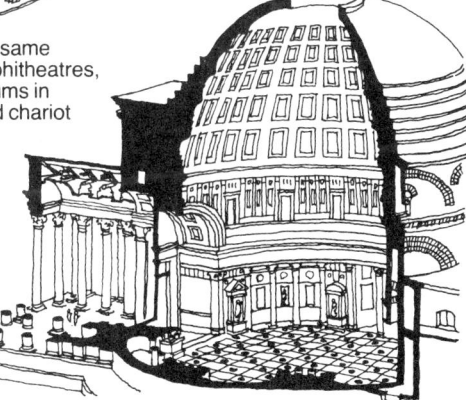

Domes were a Roman invention. They were built by putting vaulting over a circular area. This is a cut-away view of the Pantheon, a Roman temple which is now used as a church.

Gods and Goddesses

Most Roman gods and goddesses closely resembled those of the Greeks, although they had different names. The Romans also adopted other gods, from the people they conquered. In Imperial times, it became the custom to worship emperors as gods as well. The Romans believed their gods and goddesses watched over every aspect of life, although, by the 1st century BC, many of the ruling classes had begun to lose faith in them.

Juno *(Hera)*, Jupiter's wife, goddess of women and childbirth.

Minerva *(Athene)*, goddess of wisdom.

Mars *(Ares)*, god of war.

Jupiter *(Zeus)**, god of thunder and king of all the gods.

Venus *(Aphrodite)*, goddess of love and beauty.

Apollo *(Apollo)*, god of the sun.

Neptune *(Poseidon)*, god of the sea.

Ceres *(Demeter)*, goddess of corn.

Diana *(Artemis)*, goddess of the moon and hunting.

Mercury *(Hermes)*, messenger of the gods and patron of merchants.

Faunus *(Pan)* and **Flora**, god and goddess of the countryside.

Bacchus *(Dionysus)*, god of wine.

Dis Pater *(Hades)* and **Proserpine** *(Persephone)*, god and goddess of the underworld.

**The names in brackets are the Ancient Greek names.*

Mystery cults and foreign gods

By the late Republic, some Romans had lost faith in the traditional gods and found little comfort in worshipping them. So they turned to new, foreign gods, whose cults often included secret rites and ceremonies, and promised eternal joy to their worshippers.

At first, many Romans regarded these new cults with great suspicion because they often took place in secret and involved wild celebrations.

Most cults, like that of the Egyptian goddess, **Isis** (above), promised life after death for its members.

Cybele, the mother goddess from Asia Minor, was the subject of another popular cult.

The Persian sun god, **Mithras,** was worshipped by many soldiers. Women could not join his cult.

The Romans usually allowed their conquered subjects to continue worshipping their own gods. This is the British goddess, **Epona.**

Another foreign goddess was **Diana of the Ephesians,** who was different from the Roman Diana.

Sometimes a local god merged with a Roman one, like **Sul-Minerva,** goddess of the sacred spring which provided the water at Bath.

Only a few religions were outlawed, among which was that of the Druids. The Romans disapproved of their custom of human sacrifice and their plots against Roman rule, and the Druid priesthood was destroyed.

Early Christians were persecuted, as they refused to worship the emperor and were regarded as a dangerous secret society. However, their numbers grew, and in 313AD the emperor made Christianity legal.

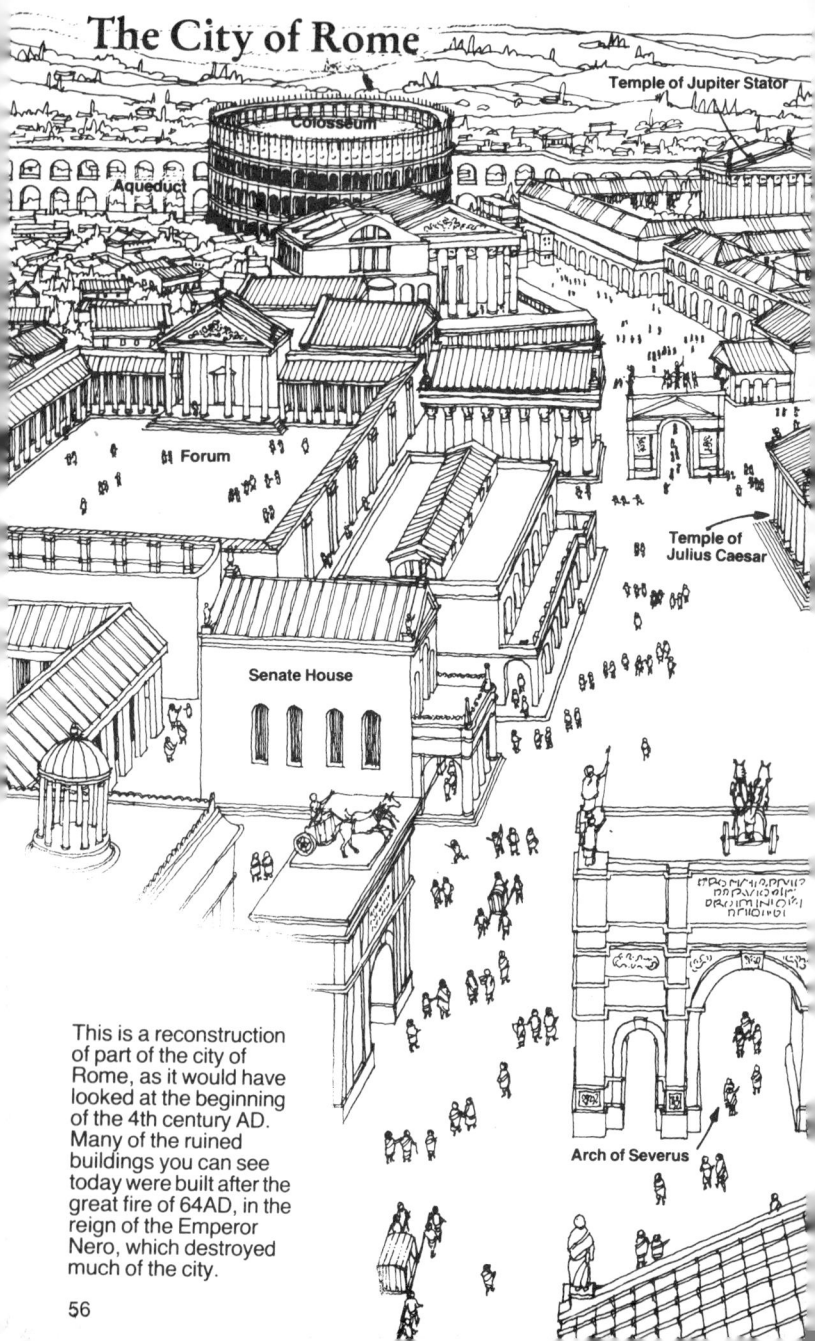

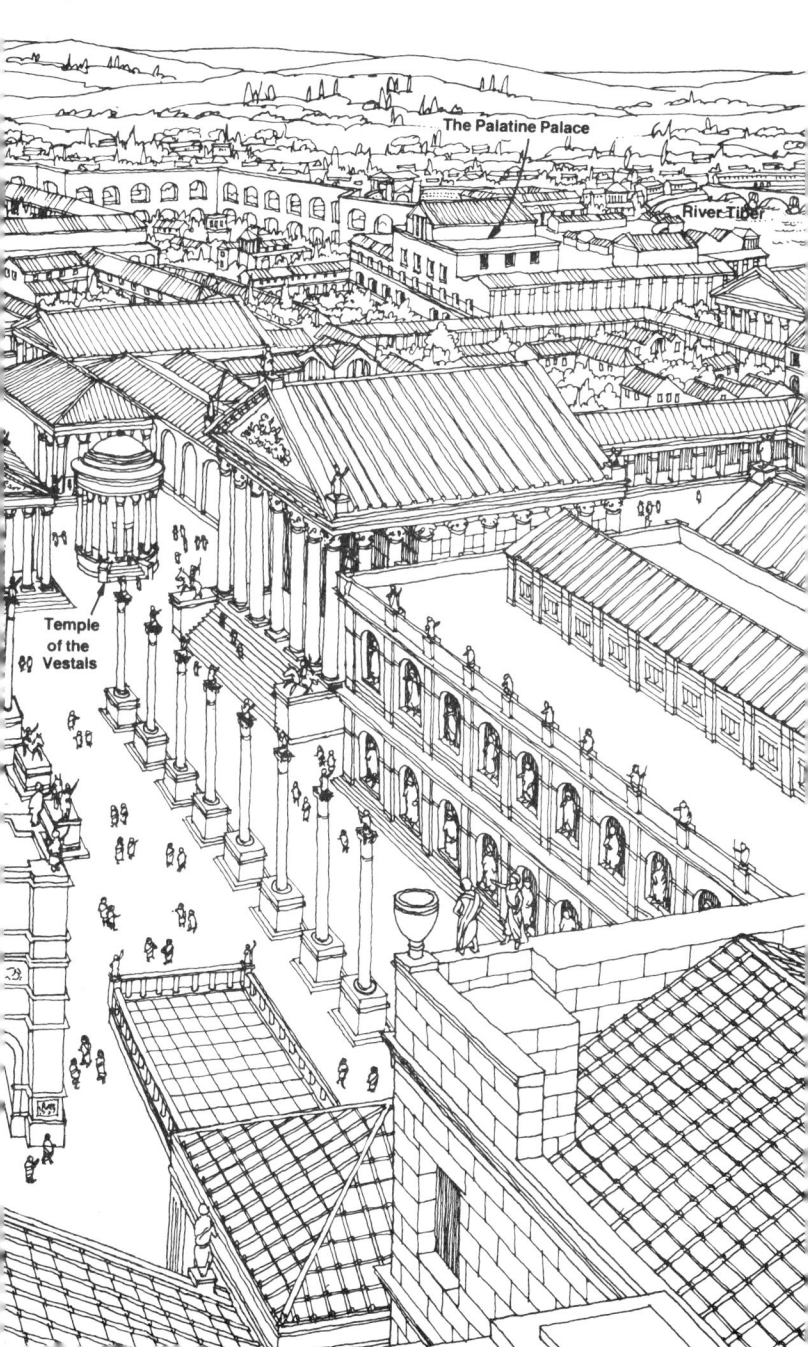

The Roman Empire

This map shows the Roman Empire at the beginning of the 2nd century AD, when it was at its largest. The Romans began by conquering the territories around their city, in order to make it safe from enemy attack. They went on to conquer other countries and gradually built up a huge empire.

Towns, roads, bridges and aqueducts were built and trade links set up. The Romans extracted taxes from their subject peoples and established a common political and legal system. The Roman language, Latin, was spoken all over the empire. In 212AD, the Emperor Caracalla gave citizenship to all the subject peoples, except slaves. Before that people had had to earn the right to citizenship.

Later, the Roman Empire was threatened by the Persians, from the south east, and by barbarians from the north east. In the 4th century AD, barbarian tribes invaded. Eventually Rome itself was captured and the Empire destroyed.

The dotted line shows the boundaries of the empire at its largest.

The provinces of the empire were ruled by governors, called proconsuls, assisted by officials and troops. Some tried to make their fortunes by over-taxing the people and keeping the extra money.

Although many settled down peacefully under Roman rule, some, like Queen Boudicca of the Iceni tribe in Britain, resented their loss of independence and rebelled.

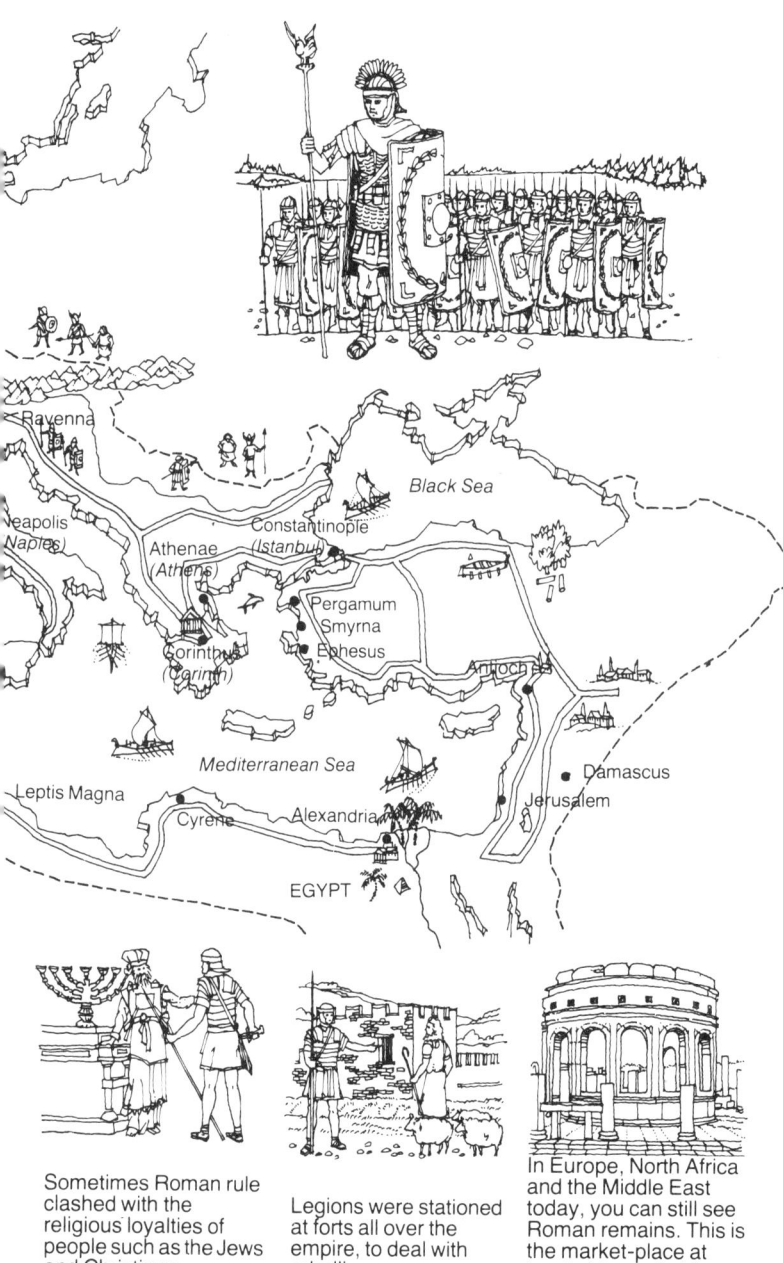

Sometimes Roman rule clashed with the religious loyalties of people such as the Jews and Christians.

Legions were stationed at forts all over the empire, to deal with rebellions.

In Europe, North Africa and the Middle East today, you can still see Roman remains. This is the market-place at Leptis Magna in Libya.

The History of Ancient Rome

According to tradition, the history of Rome dates back to 753BC. A group of farmers built fortified villages near the River Tiber in Italy. These villages eventually grew together to make a city.

Legend has it that Rome was founded by a man named Romulus. Romulus and his twin brother, Remus, had been cast out to die by a wicked uncle, but were then saved and looked after by a wolf.

Rome was ruled by kings until 510BC. The last king, Tarquin the Proud, was so unpopular that he was expelled by the people. A republic was set up and two consuls were elected each year to rule.

At first the Romans were kept busy defending themselves against powerful neighbours. As they grew in numbers and strength, they conquered more and more land around them. By 250BC, the Romans ruled all Italy and were a powerful force in the Mediterranean area.

The Romans had to fight the Carthaginians of North Africa and the Greeks, who both saw Rome as a threat to their interests. Between 264 and 146BC there were three wars with the Carthaginians. Most of the battles took place at sea.

A young Carthaginian general, called Hannibal, set out from Spain with a huge army, which included 36 elephants. They crossed the Alps into Italy, but never succeeded in capturing Rome. In 146BC, the Romans finally destroyed Carthage.

Civil war broke out in Rome as rivals fought for political power. There were riots too, as the poor plebeians demonstrated against the rich patricians. In 73BC, a slave called Spartacus led 90,000 slaves into revolt. They succeeded in fighting off the army for two years.

Two political rivals, Caesar and Pompey, struggled for control of the government. Pompey was murdered and Caesar emerged as dictator in 46BC. In 44BC he was assassinated by Brutus, Cassius and others who feared he might try to make himself king.

More civil wars followed. Caesar's great-nephew, Octavian, became the first emperor (31BC - 14AD) and changed his name to Augustus. This is the beginning of the period known as the Empire.

Augustus's family ruled as emperors until 68AD, when there were four emperors in the same year. Then came a long period of prosperity and military success under such great emperors as Vespasian, Titus, Trajan, Hadrian and Marcus Aurelius (below). The empire continued to grow in size.

By the 3rd century AD, Rome began to have problems. Rival military leaders, backed by different factions in the army, struggled to become emperor. Prices rose and the empire became hard to govern. Barbarians from the north and the east began attacking the frontiers.

The Emperor Diocletian (284–305AD) tried to stop prices rising and keep back the barbarians. Christians were often blamed for the problems and many were put to death. To make governing easier, Diocletian split the empire, so there was one emperor for the east and another for the west.

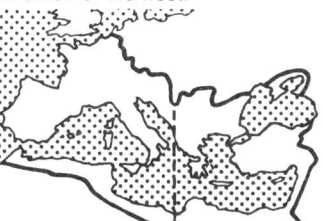

The Emperor Constantine (306–337AD) made Christianity legal. He reunited the empire and built Constantinople as its new capital. At his death, the empire was divided once more. The Eastern Empire became known as the Byzantine Empire. In the west, whole provinces were overrun by barbarians and in 410AD, Rome itself was sacked.

The western emperor and his court had already fled to Ravenna for safety. In 476AD, the last western emperor was deposed. The Eastern Empire continued to be ruled from Constantinople, until 1453AD, when it was overrun by Turks.

Museums and Sites

Here are the names of some museums where you can find interesting collections of Ancient Roman objects.

Australia

Nicholson Museum of Antiquities at the University of Sydney, Sydney, **New South Wales.**

Canada

Museum of Fine Arts, Montreal, **Quebec.**
Royal Ontario Museum, University of Toronto, Toronto, **Ontario.**

United States

Metropolitan Museum of Art, New York City, **New York.**
Museum of Fine Arts, Boston **Massachusetts.**
University Museum, University of Pennsylvania, **Philadelphia.**
Museum of Art, Cleveland, **Ohio.**
Rhode Island School of Design, Museum of Art, Providence, **Rhode Island.**

United Kingdom

In Britain, you can still see the remains of many things that the Romans built, as well as collections of Roman objects in museums. The list below (arranged in alphabetical order of countries) includes some interesting sites as well as the best museum collections.

England:
Roman Baths and Roman Baths Museum, Bath, **Avon.**
Roman amphitheatre and Grosvenor Museum, Chester, **Cheshire.**
Tullie House Museum, Carlisle, **Cumbria.**
Dorset County Museum, Dorchester, **Dorset.**
Castle Museum, Colchester, **Essex.**
Corinum Museum, Cirencester, **Gloucestershire.**
City Museum, Gloucester, **Gloucestershire.**
Chedworth Roman Villa and Museum, Yanworth, **Gloucestershire.**
District Museum, Chichester, **Hampshire.**
City Museum, Winchester, **Hampshire.**
Verulamium Roman Town and Museum, St Albans, **Hertfordshire.**
Brading Roman Villa, Brading, **Isle of Wight.**
Lullingstone Villa, Eynsford, **Kent.**
Jewry Wall Museum and Site, Leicester, **Leicestershire.**
City and County Museum, Lincoln, **Lincolnshire.**
The British Museum, London.
Museum of London, London.
Hadrian's Wall, **Northumberland.** Not all the Wall is visible. The main sites are: Chesterholm Roman Fort and Settlement, Bardon Mill; Housesteads Museum and Site, Bardon Mill; The Clayton Collection, Chesters, nr Chollerford; Corbridge Roman Station, Corbridge; Temple of Mithras, Carrawburgh.
Aldborough Roman Museum, Aldborough, **North Yorkshire.**
Rowley's House Museum, Shrewsbury, **Shropshire.**
Museum of Antiquities, The University, Newcastle, **Tyne and Wear.**
Bignor Roman Villa, Bignor, **West Sussex.**
Fishbourne Roman Palace, Fishbourne, Chichester, **West Sussex.**

Wales:
Roman Amphitheatre and Legionary Museum, Caerleon, **Gwent.**
Caerwent Roman Site, Caerwent, **Gwent.**
Segontium Roman Fort Museum, Caernarfon, **Gwynedd.**
National Museum of Wales, Cardiff, **South Glamorgan.**

Scotland:
Antonine Wall remains can be seen at Rough Castle, nr Cumbernauld, **Strathclyde.**
Hunterian Museum, Glasgow University, Glasgow, **Strathclyde.**

Index

acrobats, 26
actors, 26, 27
Aesculapius, 39
amphorae, 11
animals, 9, 10, 25, 32, 33, 38, 39, 40, 50
aqueducts, 7, 53, 56
archaeologists, 5
arches, 36, 53
architecture, 52, 53
armour, 24, 46
army, 34, 43, 46, 47, 48, 49, 50
athletes, 28
Augustus, Emperor, 9, 38, 45, 61
authors, 5, 44

bakery, 7
bandits, 50
barbarians, 58, 61
barbers, 18, 3
basilica, 52
baths, 22, 23, 42
boats, 51
books, 9, 44
Boudicca, Queen, 58
braziers, 6, 15
bridges, 37
bronze, 9, 13, 14, 15, 34, 46
buildings, 36, 43
Byzantine Empire, 61

calendar, 45
candelabrum, 15
carriages, 50
Carthaginians, 49, 60
carts, 7, 8, 50
catacombs, 41
cavalry, 47
charcoal, 11, 15
charioteers, 29
chariots, 29, 50
children, 16, 20
Christians, 25, 55, 59, 61
cities, 6
citizens, 4, 42, 43, 46, 58
cloth, 9, 35
clubs, 34
coaches, 50
coins, 9
Colosseum, 9, 24, 56
columns, 52

Constantine, Emperor, 61
Constantinople, 61
consuls, 43, 60
cooking, 8, 11, 20
copper, 9, 34
cotton, 16
couches, 12, 14
craftsmen, 20, 34, 37, 42, 52
criminals, 24, 25
crops, 32
cults, 55

dancers, 12, 24, 26
dinner parties, 3, 12, 26
Diocletian, Emperor, 61
divorce, 41
docks, 8
doctors, 45, 48
domes, 53
door handles, 10
door knockers, 10
drink, 7, 11
Druids, 55

Eastern Empire, 61
education, 20, 44, 51
eating houses, 7, 24
emperors, 9, 25, 38, 43, 45, 59, 54, 61
engineers, 48
entertainments, 24
equites, 4
exercise, 22

farmers, 20, 34
farming, 32, 33
feasts, 41
festivals, 40
fights, 24, 25
fires, 6, 15
flats, 6, 37
Flora, 40
flour, 8, 19, 34
food, 7, 8, 11, 33
forts, 49, 59
fortune-telling, 39
forum, 5, 8, 52
fountains, 7, 30
freed men and women, 4, 26, 27, 29
funerals, 41
furniture, 9, 14

Games, the, 24, 25, 40, 42, 43

games, 21, 28
gardens, 10, 22, 23, 30, 31
gladiators, 24, 25
glass, 13, 34
goddesses, 5, 38, 39, 40, 54
gods, 5, 31, 38, 39, 40, 45, 54
gold, 9, 13, 14, 18, 25, 29, 50
government, 34, 42, 43
Greeks, 17, 20, 28, 44, 45, 52, 60
guard dogs, 10
gymnasiums, 22

Hadrian, Emperor, 49
hairdressers, 18, 23
Hannibal, 60
heating, 15, 22
herbs, 11, 33
Herculaneum, 5
historians, 5
holidays, 24, 40, 51
hospitals, 48
houses, 10, 31
hunting, 28, 33
hypocaust, 15

Ides of March, 9
illness, 39
inns, 50
inspectors, 9
iron, 34
ivory, 14, 18, 50

jewellery, 17
Jews, 25, 59
jobs, 34, 35
jugglers, 24, 26
Julius Caesar, Emperor, 9, 45, 46, 61

keys, 10
kitchen, 7

labourers, 34, 42, 48
lamps, 8, 15
lanterns, 15
lavatories, 7, 24
law, 44, 45
laws, 43
leather, 17, 33, 46
legends, 5
libraries, 21, 22, 23
linen, 16

litters, 50
locks, 10
luxuries, 9

make-up, 19
manumission, 42
marble, 14, 22, 37
markets, 8, 43
massage, 23
medicine, 39, 45
mills, 8, 34
money, 9, 49
moneylenders, 9
mosaics, 3, 31, 37
musical instruments, 26
musicians, 3, 12, 24, 26

Nero, Emperor, 56
night-watchmen, 6
nobles, 34
non-citizens, 4, 42, 47
numbers, 45
nurses, 20

oil, 8, 11, 15, 23, 33
oratory, 21, 44

paintings, 5, 30, 31, 37
Pantheon, the, 3, 53
papyrus, 20, 44
parties, 12, 16, 19, 26
patricians, 4, 43
patrons, 42, 44
pavements, 7
pay, 48, 49
perfume, 9, 19
Persians, 58
philosophers, 44
pirates, 51
plays, 26, 27
playwrights, 12
plebeians, 4, 34, 42, 43, 60
poets, 5, 12, 44
politics, 43, 44
Pompeii, 5, 10
Pompey, 61
portraits, 5
pottery, 13, 15, 35
Praetorian Guard, 49
priests, 24, 38, 39, 48
priestesses, 24, 38, 39
processions, 24, 40, 41, 49
proconsuls, 43, 58
professions, 44
provinces, 4, 43, 58

punishments, 45, 48

rents, 6, 33
roads, 50, 51
Roman Empire, 4, 58, 59
Romulus and Remus, 40, 60

sacrifices, 38, 39, 55
Saturn, 40
scales, 9
schools, 20
sculptors, 37
sculptures, 30
Senate, 43
servants, 42
sewers, 7
ships, 49, 51
shops, 6, 8, 9, 22
shrines, 38, 39
siege, 48
silk, 16
silver, 9, 13, 14, 50
slaves, 4, 8, 11, 12, 18, 19, 20, 22, 23, 24, 25, 26, 29, 32, 34, 35, 36, 40, 42, 44, 50, 58, 60
soldiers, 20, 46, 47, 48, 49
Spartacus, 60
spices, 11, 19
spinning, 20
sports, 21, 28
statues, 14, 22, 30, 37, 38
stores, 11,
surveyors, 48, 51
Sybil, the, 39

tableware, 13
Tarquin the Proud, King, 60
taverns, 7
taxes, 58
teachers, 20, 44
temples, 38, 52
theatres, 26, 27, 53
togas, 16, 42
tombs, 41
towns, 52
tortoise-shell, 14
toys, 21
traders, 9, 34, 42, 51
transport, 50, 51
travel, 17, 50, 51
tribunes, 43

tumblers, 24
tutors, 20

vases, 30
vaults, 36, 53
Vesta, 38, 39
Vestal virgins, 39, 40
Vesuvius, 5
villas, 30, 31, 32

warehouses, 8
warfare, 46
water, 7
water wheels, 34
weapons, 24, 46, 48
weddings, 41
wild animals, 25
wine, 11, 33
women, 16, 18, 19, 34, 35, 41
wood, 14, 19, 50
wool, 14, 16